CONTENTS

Any words appearing in the text in bold, **like this**, are explained in the Glossary.

Why don't gorillas lay eggs?

WHY DON'T GORILLAS LAY EGGS?

By Katherine Smith

Consultant: Nicola Davies

ticktock
M E D I A

WHY DON'T GORILLAS LAY EGGS?

Copyright © *ticktock* Entertainment Ltd 2004

First published in Great Britain in 2004 by *ticktock* Media Ltd.,

Unit 2, Orchard Business Centre, North Farm Road, Tunbridge Wells, Kent, TN2 3XF

We would like to thank: Meme Ltd and Elizabeth Wiggans.

ISBN 1 86007 515 0 PB

ISBN 1 86007 519 3 HB

Printed in China

A CIP catalogue record for this book is available from the British Library.

Because gorillas are **mammals**. Like most mammals, they give birth to live babies.

Just like human babies, baby gorillas need lots of love and care from their mothers. They stay with their mums for many years, learning how to look after themselves, and how to treat others.

Baby gorillas feed on their mother's milk.

Baby gorillas start to crawl at about six months old. They can walk by the time they are three years old.

Gorillas usually have just one baby at a time.

Young male gorillas leave their family groups when they are about 11 years old to build nests of their own.

Mothers carry their young around, to keep them safe from danger.

Why don't gorillas have long tails?

Because gorillas are apes, not monkeys.

Only monkeys have tails. Gorillas belong to the great **ape** family, along with orang-utans, chimpanzees, and bonobos. Apes have long arms, hands, and feet that can grab hold of things.

Gorillas have very good eyesight, and can see in colour.

Orang-utans are the only great apes that don't live in groups.

Like all apes, gorillas are clever. They use their brains to work out the answers to problems.

Gorillas' arms are longer than their legs.

Why don't gorillas have colourful coats?

Because gorillas like to stay hidden in the forest.

Some gorillas have thicker fur to keep warm.

Gorillas are shy, peaceful creatures. Their dark coats make them hard to spot in the lush **rain forests** where they live. This is called **camouflage**.

Gorillas have no hair on their chest, palms, nose, ears, lips, or the soles of their feet.

Some gorillas live in cold mountain forests.
They have thicker coats to keep warm.

Baby gorillas have a white
tail tuft on their bottoms.
This helps their mothers find
them in the rain forests.

Why don't gorillas like to live on their own?

Because gorillas are very sociable animals.

Female gorillas and their babies live, eat, play, travel, and sleep in groups called **harems**. Adult male gorillas are called **silverbacks**. Each group of gorillas has one silverback that takes charge and defends the group from danger.

Adult males have a silver patch of fur on their backs. This is where they get the name "silverback" from.

When danger threatens, the silverback will roar, scream, beat his chest, and finally charge at his enemies.

The head male is twice the size of a female gorilla.

Gorillas groom one another as a way of being friendly. It also helps to keep them free of fleas and other insects.

19

Why don't gorillas need umbrellas when it rains?

20

Because gorillas build their own SHELTERS.

Just like humans, gorillas don't like to get wet in the rain. Instead, they cleverly bend branches and leaves down over their heads to make a shelter.

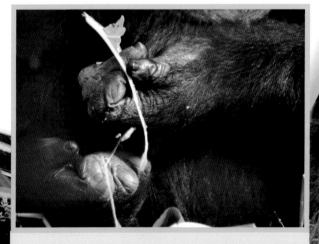

Having fingers and toes helps gorillas pick things up and build shelters.

Gorillas build a nest of fresh grass and leaves every day, to sleep in at night.

Gorilla fur is not waterproof, but it does protect them from the cold.

Why don't gorillas eat hamburgers?

Because gorillas are herbivores, and don't eat meat.

There's nothing a gorilla likes better
than a tasty meal of fruit, shoots,
roots, tree bark, and leaves.
In fact, gorillas need to spend
a lot of the day eating,
to give them energy.

Gorillas do not
need to drink
water because
they get water
from the fruit and
leaves they eat.

Although they are **herbivores**, gorillas sometimes eat grubs and **termites** too.

Gorillas can grip with their hands. This allows them to pick up food.

Gorillas help make the forest grow. Their droppings contain the plant seeds they have eaten.

27

Gorilla **Profile**

Life span

Up to 35 years.

Size

1.8 metres – that's about as tall as a man!

Weight

Up to 163 kilos – that's twice as heavy as a man!

Numbers

There are an estimated 50,000 gorillas living in the wild.

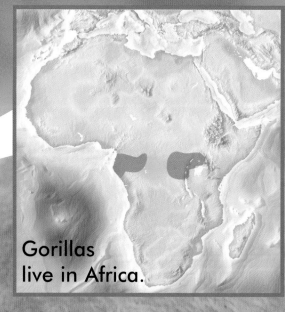

Gorillas
live in Africa.

Fact file

There are five different types of gorilla:

The **mountain** gorilla

The **Bwindi Forest** gorilla

The **eastern lowland** gorilla

The **western lowland** gorilla

The **Cross River** gorilla

Gorillas are an **endangered species**. There are only 650 mountain gorillas left in the world!

Gorillas will attack if threatened, but are gentle with people if they are kind to them.

GLOSSARY

Ape
An animal such as a chimpanzee or gorilla that is closely related to human beings and has no tail.

Camouflage
Colourings or markings on an animal or insect that allows it to blend in with its natural surroundings.

Endangered species
A species of animal that is in danger of being hunted by human beings or of losing its habitat (the place where it lives).

Harem
The name for a group of female gorillas.

Herbivore	An animal that does not eat meat.
Mammals	Animals that are warm-blooded and produce milk for their young.
Rain forest	A thick, bushy forest in a tropical area that has an annual rainfall of at least 100 inches.
Silverback	An adult male gorilla that is in charge of a harem. It has a silver patch of fur on its back.
Termites	Small ant-like insects found in hot, rainy areas.

INDEX